Habits of the Super Rich

Proven Ways to Make Money, Get Rich, and Be Successful

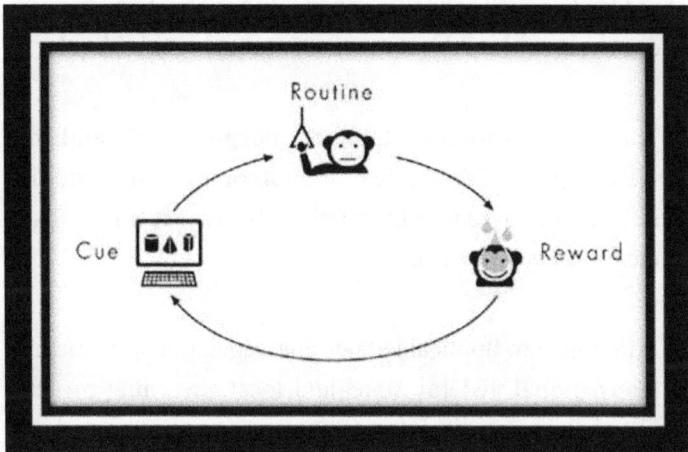

Bruce Walker

CONTENTS

BRUCE WALKER

Chapter 4: The Universal Laws of Success............41

The Law of Attraction...42
The Law of Allowing..47
The Law of Resistance......................................50
The Law of Detachment 52
The Law of Abundance....................................55
Using the Law of Abundance to
Your Advantage Right Now 59
The Law of Action 60
Create your Very Own Fantasy World 64
Take this Habit to the Next Level......................65

Chapter 5: The Powerful Habit of a
Mastermind Group 70

Chapter 6: The Most Effective Way to
Build a Habit..78
Add a Habit . . . Subtract What?.......................82
How long does it take to instill a habit? 85

Chapter 7: Become Aware of your Surroundings...89
Meet Others of Like Minds................................93

Chapter 8: Meditation: A Habit of 85% of all
Successful people 102
Should You Meditate?......................................105

Conclusion 114
You're only Laying the Foundation.................116

INTRODUCTION

"The rich get richer, while the poor get poorer."
"If you're not born rich, you'll never get rich."
"It's impossible to be successful today, there's just too much competition."

H ave you heard – or even repeated – any of these adages? If you have, you're not alone. All of us have felt that way at one time or another. But if you take them to heart and say them day after day, they become ingrained in your subconscious and you begin to believe them. These words, which seemed harmless enough when you first started saying them, may have now become a self-fulfilling prophecy.

When that happens, you think that everyone else is successful, regardless of how you define your personal success, but you. The ironic aspect of this is that you can try all sorts of measures from investing in the stock market to online marketing to multi-layer marketing, to – yes! – even playing the lottery. None of these works. At the end of the day, month or year, you haven't seemed to make any more money or be any more successful in your career than when you first starting working toward your goal.

Actually, that's not surprising. Some individuals call the use of this mantra so that it's part of your belief system a "self-fulfilling prophecy." It's also known as a "poverty" mentality. They don't have the ability to see themselves as being successful. We all know people like this. Regardless of how hard they work, just they seem to have "bad luck."

Those who have even worked hard in order to work up the economic ladder find, at times, that their mindset holds them back. Imagine a single mom with several children who worked three jobs just to make ends meet. As they grew and she was able to she took courses to become a registered nurse. Today she makes a great income, but still hoards her paycheck and won't pay a utility bill until the companies send a representative to turn off the utility. She has never recovered from her "poverty mentality."

Then there's the other end of the spectrum: the individual who seems to be able to make all the mistakes in the world and still come out successful. No matter what he does he ends up "smelling like roses," as they say.

The Difference Between The Rich and The Poor

In one word: habits!

You can set all the goals you want. To earn $125,000 a year or more. To get that promotion at work. To become a New York Times bestselling author. But unless you have established good habits you'll never reach those goals. Unless you establish the habits of "the rich and famous" you'll forever be chasing success and it will be just slightly out of your grasp.

The real truth is that you can have all the riches and success – however, you define them – you wish. There really are no limits to what you can achieve. All you have to do is change your "poverty" mentality to one of success. All you need to do is change the habits that keep you chained to your current lifestyle and your current salary. Swap these habits for better ones, for habits and thoughts and insights that will make you as rich, as successful, as happy as you care to be.

If you're serious about climbing the rungs of success at your workplace, in any online venture or in the entrepreneurial world, then you can do it. And you can accomplish this simply by turning a few bad habits into a few good habits.

The Power of Imitation

That's where this book comes in. This book can succinctly and easily help you recognize and implement those habits the rich and famous use in order to achieve and maintain success. Consider this volume your personal "how-to" manual to getting what you desire out of life.

This book is actually only one in a long lineage of classic self-help books. Books like this have been published for years. Probably the most famous is Napoleon Hill's *Think and Grow Rich* or more recently Jack Canfield's *The Success Principles.* If his name sounds familiar, it should. He was one of the editors of the wildly successful books, the first of which was called *Chicken Book for the Soul*. Since then, he and his co-editor Mark Hansen have built that book into a franchise.

Think and Grow Rich author Hill was commissioned by Andrew Carnegie to discover the common habits and traits of the highly successful industrialists of the early twentieth century.

The truth of the matter is that if you visit a book-store or go to any website that sells books, you'll discover a myriad of self-help books all promising to make you rich.

So why does the world need another book on this topic, this one specifically? Because few, if any, of the reputable books on this topic, are written this succinctly. This well-written book gets to the crux of the issue, not only letting you know what the best habits are, how they work and how you can use them to help you "think and grow rich" yourself. In a conversational tone, this volume explains why habits are so very important and how you can effortlessly adopt them.

Not only that, but this book is easy to keep near you, either on your computer desktop, on your ebook reader or both. This means you can refer to it whenever you find your spirit sagging or a dark cloak of pessimism trying to smother you. In these cases, it's easy to pull out this book for inspiration. Before you know, you'll back on track, practicing the good habits all successful individuals do – and knowing that all the universal laws are working toward your success.

It incorporates all the ideas of the classic writers as well as the best of the ideas from today's motivational speakers and books.

What You'll Discover in this Book

This book will show you the habits of the successful and help you put them into practice so that they'll become second nature to you. Not only that, but along with those habits, you'll learn why these habits work, starting with the Universal laws of success. They come in many forms, including the recently celebrated Law of Attraction. Many of you may already be familiar with this from the movie and book, *The Secret.*

In addition to the law of attraction, there are several other laws that go hand-in-hand with it that can solidify your success for you. These laws a bit less well-known, the laws of detachment, allowing, abundance and gratitude – to name just a few.

You'll also learn the science behind why these habits and perfectly enmeshed. It all starts with the subconscious mind. Equipped with this information, you can go out and initiate any good habit and within the period of your choice, have it become a part of you.

You don't think any of this is possible? Do you still believe that only a few, the privileged deserve success? If you still think you're "condemned" to live an ordinary life yearning for more, then you need to start reading this book right now.

In the first chapter, you'll vividly see the habits you choose to use can either make or break your success. Why not dig in right now and begin your well-deserved journey to success?

There's no time like the present to change your thinking from "the rich only get richer" to "I am prosperous beyond my wildest imagination."

CHAPTER 1:

❧

HABITS OF THE RICH AND THE POOR

Jim and Zach had been friends since high school. Both were straight-A students. In fact, they graduated sharing the honors as co-valedictorians. There was only one major difference between them, though. Jim didn't need to study. His talent was natural and he soon discovered that a quick look at his lessons was all he needed to get his "A." After that, he turned his attention to recreational pursuits.

Zach, on the other hand, worked hard to keep up with Jim's natural abilities. He found that he needed to study in order to get his good grades. He naturally searched for, developed and perfected habits to help him do just that. Zach knew when to say no to a social invitation in order to study for that *important exam, even though it meant missing the good times of a few social engagements.*

Throughout their high school career, Jim chided Zach in a good-natured tone about his apparent discipline and the acquisition of his many study habits. Jim took it all in stride saying, "I'll do whatever it takes to get good grades."

Then the pair went off to the same college. It was then Zach's turn to tease his best friend Jim/ Zach was able to take the same habits he had developed in high school and apply them to his college courses.

It's not that Jim was a bad student. Not by any stretch of the imagination. Especially during his first two years. He was able to breeze through the courses, just as he had done in high school.

However, as he got into upper-level coursework he had a bit of trouble here and there. Zach, could see that Jim's academic career may be in danger if he didn't adopt some solid positive habits – and soon.

When graduation day came, Zach had a higher grade point average than Jim. Not by much, but by enough.

As luck would have it, Zach and John received job offers from the same corporation. They worked side by side for several years. But now the tables were turned. Those positive habits Zach had developed in high school and used in college were now the same ones that he needed to prove himself at work.

Jim, though, found it difficult to adjust to the business world. He had not created any good habits during his educational career. In fact, in college, he probably adopted more bad habits than anything else.

Can you guess which proved the better employee? Bingo! Zach. Even though he had to work at everything he did, his habits, by this time, came so naturally to him, that it didn't seem like so much work.

What was worse was that the bad habits Jim had acquired in college carried over to his professional career. Little by little he discovered that he was on a downward spiral.

Bad Habits and the Downward Spiral

If you've never heard of that notorious downward spiral before, think of it like that "slippery slope" so many individuals love to talk about. Let's take the habit of "punctuality," or showing up on time for work. We all can point to someone who is chronically late – to church, to social events, to appointments. While that's irritating, being late to those events isn't career-threatening.

Then there are those who are chronically late for work. These are the people who are most at risk of experiencing that downward spiral. You wouldn't think one small habit of being on time could possibly be that crucial in a job. But you'd be surprised where even one small, unassuming bad habit could lead.

If someone were late for work every morning even by ten minutes, his supervisor would eventually note that. Perhaps he may even issue him warnings about it. His supervisor may overlook it if the person were outstanding in his job. But, what if, the individual had the same bad habit of being late in meeting deadlines at work? Turning reports in late, being late to vital meetings – even those that kept important clients waiting.

There's only so much an employer will tolerate. Before you know it, the employer has fired this individual. Think that's the lowest down a spiral can go? Think again. The journey continues. During the time he's off work, he can't find a job, he has trouble meeting his bills and, well, it only goes downhill from there.

All for the lack of one good habit: punctuality.

Let's now look at the flip side of that single habit. Let's assume that this employee, instead, came to work on time every day. How would his career have changed?

Had he done this, his employer would have no need to even give him a warning.

Additionally, if this employee had practiced punctuality, he would have naturally been on time – perhaps even early – for all meetings, turning in all reports and especially for those vital meetings with the company's most important clients.

The Upward Spiral

In the end, he probably would have been a shining example of a model employee and would have been in line for a promotion. With just that one small change in habit, he could have gone from his modest position to a much more lucrative and more responsible position.

There's no need to tell you that as part of that upward spiral, his budding career would have included several salary increases along the way. This means that his personal life also would have been on an upward spiral of a larger house and everything he and his family needed and wanted to create the ideal family life.

Punctuality is just one habit successful people have. If you study the habits of the successful, like the authors Napoleon Hill and later Steven Covey did, you'll find that they hold many of the same good habits.

If you feel as if your life is stagnant and you haven't had the joy of the upward spiral – or worse yet, you recognize you're on that downward spiral -- you may be motivated to seriously scrutinize your habits – right here and right now.

Changing the Direction of the Spiral

Some of us have the mistaken belief that those individuals who have struck it rich and succeeded beyond belief have done so using "dumb luck." That couldn't be farther from the truth, if you scratch the surface, what you discover just below their shiny success, are years of their practicing ingrained good habits.

The good news is that you too can adopt the same habits which made them wildly successful – and become as successful as you desire.

Before you say that it's impossible to change your habits, let's move on to chapter two, which talks about the miraculous power of your subconscious mind and how, with even just a bit of effort, it'll help you not only stop the downward spiral you may find yourself in right now, but actually help you turn the tide and start on an upward spiral.

CHAPTER 2:

꙳

TURNING THOUGHTS INTO REALITY: IT ALL STARTS WITH THE SUBCONSCIOUS MIND

The ancestor of every action is a thought.
--Ralph Waldo Emerson

Jim and Zach, our friends from the first chapter, we're talking one day. By this point in their careers, Zach was on the fast track – his upward spiral – toward an upper management job.

Jim, on the other hand, was experiencing a downward spiral – and he seemed to be plummeting down that rabbit hole quicker than Alice in Wonderland.

For his part, Jim was in shock, wondering how he could have gotten himself into such a position. "Can I speak honestly with you," Zach offered. After receiving his consent, his pal outlined exactly what he saw.

Jim took a deep breath and said. "It looks pretty hopeless," he said.

Zach immediately corrected him. "It's never hopeless. That is if you're willing to put in some time and effort." Jim immediately agreed.

"Once you take the first step, your subconscious mind will help you the rest of the way."

It's a very simple concept, but one that we tend to overlook. It's one, though, that our friend Zach seemed to know.

When we do acknowledge it we simply underrate it. But it's true. Every building constructed, every book written, every business created first began as some one's thoughts.

Many individuals believe that there's no understanding of the subconscious mind. They know ideas pop into their heads, seemingly miraculously, in the middle of the night. They also know that if they don't write them down they seem to dematerialize into a thin cloud of smoke never to be remembered again. The workings of the mind are a mystery, they believe. It's a magical, mystical mystery tour.

Ask anyone who thought with great confidence that they would surely remember this life-changing concept that woke them up without warning at two in the morning. They smiled, simply rolled over and went back to sleep. When the alarm woke them up at 7 a.m., they were so close to recalling the idea . . . but couldn't.

What is the Subconscious Mind?

Your subconscious mind is the repository of the myriad of information that flies by us every day even if we're not aware of them. Our mind catches them in mid-flight and files them away. It's amazing how much information the subconscious mind stores for us, even if we aren't aware we have it stored away somewhere.

But here's a secret about the subconscious that few know. It works best when we're not aware of it working. It's at its most efficient when we aren't alert. That's why we wake up with those wonderful ideas at times. When we sleep we don't have a clue as to what that portion of the mind is doing.

Similarly, it works its magic when we are doing something totally unrelated to what we're working on. How many times have you walked away from a problem or a glitch in a project to have the answer flash in front of you?

No doubt you're well aware of those moments. They may differ from person to person, they may even differ for you depending on the problem and the situation. That's why the eureka moment hits you when you're taking a shower, watching television or even driving a car.

Ever get in a car and drive through an intersection wondering if you really stopped at that red light? Or maybe while you're driving you actually forget to turn on the proper street. That's your subconscious mind working out the details of a project or problem for you.

Ask just about any writer and he'll tell you he gets his best ideas as soon as he opens his eyes in the morning.

Remember those days in grade school and high school when the teacher admonished you for daydreaming? The implication was that you were wasting your time. These days you probably should be doing more of it. Yes, daydreaming is a wonderful way of exercising your subconscious mind. Others find they can put the subconscious mind to work through hypnosis.

The secret about the subconscious mind that all successful people know is that you can use this portion of your brain to your advantage instead of being at the mercy of its seemingly whimsical nature. Through the deliberate use of the subconscious mind, you can use your mind more effectively to influence not only your motivation, but your willpower as well. In fact, once you begin to train yourself in the proper procedure of using this portion of your mind, you'll discover that there's not much you can't do.

How Successful People Put the Subconscious to Work

The following are facts every successful person knows about the subconscious mind. Not only does he know these facts, but he also works within their bounds so he can make the most of this awesome power.

Subconscious Mind Fact #1: The subconscious mind has no agenda of its own.

This layer of your mind has no will of its own. It doesn't have a "hidden agenda" that is trying to persuade you to its side of an argument or perspective. It's one and only one function:

The subconscious exists solely to produce ideas according to the beliefs and the images you place in it.

Unlike other areas of our brain, such as the ego or the conscious mind, it doesn't judge these images, beliefs or thoughts. Sounds pretty good, doesn't it? You might be thinking right about now that it should be your best friend.

Indeed it should. But then you have to learn that because it doesn't judge, it will manifest anything you place into it. That means it will as readily give you the lack of money you've been thinking about as well as the prosperity you desire. The subconscious mind will hand you illness as quickly as it will hand you health.

To put it in more concrete terms, your subconscious mind is essentially working off the blueprint of your life that you're feeding – whether you realize it or not. It won't stop to examine your thoughts and censor out the negative ones then chastise you for thinking them.

The subconscious mind receives all that you feed it, then begins to bring them to life. Think about it! It could be an awesome tool. If you're thinking prosperity, visualizing the life you dream of, it's not about to judge you. Instead, it quietly goes to work bringing it about. In this way, Emerson was right on the mark. A thought really is the ancestor of every action.

The opposite of this is true as well though. If you go to bed at night – or spend the best part of your day – worrying over your debts, affirming that you live from paycheck to paycheck, then what do you believe your subconscious will deliver you on a silver platter. Exactly what you've been thinking about: more debt.

Instead of finding that fact depressing, you should view it as liberating. Just by changing what you think about – especially right before you go to bed at night and as soon as you wake up in the morning – can actually be the catalyst for the successful life you've been hungering for.

Napoleon Hill knew this when in the 1930s he wrote *Think and Grow Rich.* After interviewing the most productive and most successful business people of his day, he recognized how to use the subconscious mind to produce success. In his book, he speaks about manifesting "riches" into your life, this same six-step process, based on the nonjudgmental actions of the subconscious mind, can work the same type of magic in your life that it did for others – bring them untold success.

Napoleon Hill's proven Six-Step Process to Success

1. Decide on the specific amount of money you want

This is a very important step. When Hill writes "exact amount" he means it. The more specific you can be in your mind, the better. Don't be wishy-washy about this. Don't waffle. Just decide on how much you want.

Notice I didn't say "need." Don't make the mistake many individuals do at this point in the process. They don't decide on enough. Catherine Ponder a motivational speaker once said, "It's as easy to manifest a button as it is to a castle."

Do yourself a favor from the very beginning, never settle for the button when you really want the castle.

2. Decide what you're going to give in return for receiving this money.

Many people expect at this point money will just rain down from heaven for them, just like in the Old Testament story of the Hebrews in the desert and the manna or bread. Don't expect that you're going to receive your riches by hitting the lottery. Be prepared to start working on an idea – if you haven't already.

Are you going to start offering your services as a writer? Or are you going to start an online business? Now is the time to follow your passion.

3. Establish a deadline.

Go ahead, don't be afraid. You're not going to insult your subconscious mind by presenting it with a deadline. If you don't do this, you'll discover that these "riches" or whatever you desire will always be just out of your reach.

4. Make a detailed plan of action.

Again, don't expect these riches just to fall from heaven. Don't expect your business plan to materialize in front of you with the wave of a magic wand. Instead, you'll want to write out in detail how you plan to carry out your business or your services.

Remember, every good business person started off this way. Think of it as a map. You're here, where "x" marks the spot. There's no use decrying where you are at the moment. Just accept this is your location and your resources for the moment and know – without any reservation of doubt – that you will get to exactly where you'll want to be.

You want to be here, where the map indicates the "treasure" is waiting for you. Besides, a well thought out business plan is the first thing any bank asks for when a person requests a business loan. Where do you plan to be in the next five years? How do you plan to acquire your riches?

That's right. Get a pen and paper. It's better, by the way, to do this initially in long-hand instead of on a computer. This makes it seem more of a serious commitment. Make sure when you do this you include all the necessary facts. This includes the exact amount of money you intend to manifest in your life. Give it a deadline, then write down what services you're going to provide in return for this money. Not only that, but accurately detail the plan you have for bringing all of this to fruition. At this point, you may believe you're done. Not quite.

6. Read this statement twice a day.

Use the power of the spoken word and spend time reading your written account twice a day. Make of a habit of doing this first thing in the morning, before you place any other ideas in your mind and again in the evening, so it's the last idea you think about before going to bed.

But here's the catch. When you do read it, visualize it your mind. Feel the excitement of success coursing through your body. Believe that the riches you desire, the business you're willing to build to receive it are already manifest in your life. In other words, believe with all the fiber of your body that you already have the money.

TRUTH #2 – The Subconscious can't tell the real from the imagined

For such a potentially powerful organ, the subconscious seems to be "naive." It can't tell the real from the imagined, it only "lives" in the present and understands the present. When people first learn these facts, they try to deny them. After all, your mind is so miraculous, it seems incredulous you can manipulate it so easily.

Think about what was just said. "You can manipulate it – the subconscious mind – so easily." Again, this is difficult to believe. But once you can overcome your disbelief, you may begin to kick yourself. After all, if this is true, then why didn't you learn this earlier in life? It seems like a fairly simple method to help kick-start your success.

As we learn to work with this portion of the brain and learn habits of the rich and famous, you'll discover how important this concept is to your own overcoming bad habits, acquiring good ones and marching forward to success.

TRUTH #3 – The Subconscious only understands the present

The key to true success lies in the "present tense." When you start giving instructions to your brain, you're always going to talk to it in the present tense. When you write out your affirmations, they'll always be written in the present tense. Have you gone through Napoleon Hill's six steps yet? If you have, stop right here and review them. Make sure everything you want is phrased in the present tense. Don't use the future tense.

By now you can probably guess what that would do. That would mean you can see your riches, but they would always be just beyond your reach because you keep asking for them in the future. The future never arrives. By the time it gets here, we call it today. Again, the subconscious is a literal creature.

How Did you get to this Point?

Let's take a step back here for a moment. We should rephrase this. Theoretically, it should be easy to manipulate your subconscious. The problem for many of us, if not all of us, is that others have already manipulated it before we even thought to do this was possible.

Or perhaps you've had a hand in manipulating it yourself and now you have to undo the "damage." What do we mean by that? Perhaps you've been told by your parents growing up that you're not going to succeed in a certain occupation. The competition is fierce and, quite frankly, you're just not smart enough. Think about the field day your subconscious mind had with that statement.

The results? Two possible ones could have manifested. First, you may have avoided that vocation altogether believing that you would never succeed. Or perhaps you were smart enough to ignore your parents and enter the occupation of your dreams only to find yourself failing desperately in it. Why? Because your subconscious mind was already imprinted with the thoughts of failure.

TRUTH #3 - Habits Are the Footprints of the Subconscious

This is an elaborate way of saying that all of your habits are dictated by your subconscious mind. Depending on your point of view, this could be good news or bad news.

Habits are just actions that have been ingrained into our system – some of them since childhood. Think about the habit of brushing your teeth. When you were a youngster your parents probably drilled into you the necessity of that habit. It wasn't something your mind told you to do. But one day, after your parents reminded you for so long, something in your mind clicked. Your parents no longer needed to remind you – and it became a habit.

Ask any person who works at home for a living. These individuals had to establish good habits in order to keep on track every day. These activities are dictated by their job. If it weren't for these "work habits" they never would have been able to sustain such a thriving business.

The truth be told, habits drive all successful people and the subconscious mind drives habits. In order to change your bad habits into good ones, you'll have to manipulate your subconscious. We've already seen that given the attributes of the mind, what may sound difficult, may actually be much easier than you think.

Exercises to Direct the Power of your Subconscious

The beauty of the power of your subconscious is that it is easily trainable. For the longest time, the majority of individuals seeking success were unaware of the power of this awesome aspect of the mind. We thought our bad luck was just that "bad luck." We thought our limited income was somehow dictated by the gods of prosperity or by some fundamental lack of currency in the world.

Neither of these concepts would be further from the truth. Are you ready to start training your subconscious mind to work for you, to bring you your deepest desires, including success in your career and the prosperity that accompanies that, great relationships – both professional and personal – and the power to dictate your moods?

If you've personalized the six steps of Napoleon Hill's found earlier in this chapter, congratulations. You've already taken the first step. But just like exercising any other muscles, you have to perform a variety of exercises to create the habits you'll need in order to get what you want.

The following three exercises will help you reach your goals. You can start using these immediately, while you're reading and studying the rest of this book.

Subconscious Exercise 1: Create Your Vision of a Successful life

Prior to reading this book you probably didn't realize you were the person responsible for the financial or emotional state of your life at this very moment. You may have wanted to blame it on being in the wrong place at the wrong time or a lack of money or even a lack of love.

As we move forward in these chapters you'll learn about the law of abundance. Succinctly this universal law states that there is no lack in the universe, but only an abundance. And it really doesn't matter an abundance of what. You can live the life you've been dreaming of without depriving someone else of their abundant and rich vision of their life. Once you quit thinking that this life is a competition among everyone else you meet or even a rat race, you'll be amazed at how doors, once locked, open easily to your touch.

Even before you learn the workings of this law, you can put it to use. Simply visualize the life you want. That's right! Instead of dwelling on the vision of your life as it is now, begin to imagine the life you want to lead. See it now: the ideal career, the ideal house, the ideal family.

But don't just see it, feel it with every fiber of your body. Get excited about what you're seeing. Feel as if you were living it right now.

Start this visualization process now, and when we talk more about this in a later chapter you'll be that much farther along in the process and, of course, closer to your goals.

When is the best time to visualize? Right before you go to sleep at night and as soon as you wake up in the morning.

Exercise 2: Write Your 10 Goals Daily

Imagine this statistic. Less than three percent of Harvard University students have set goals. At one of the most competitive schools in the nation, that seems to be a small percentage of the students.

Yet, we know that one of the most effective ways to get where you want to go and to enjoy your success is through the creation of goals. If you've thought about setting written goals, you should consider it right now.

Do more than just consider it, though. You should write them down. Think about all the daydreams you've had since you were a child. Consider what you would be doing today if you knew you couldn't fail. If you knew that you could take that leap of faith and succeed, what would you be doing with your life?

Take ten of these goals and write them done. Now, read these out loud several times a day. You may already be a step ahead of me knowing that two of these recitations should be before you go to bed at night and when you wake up in the morning.

Now, take the first step toward one of these goals. You'll see almost immediately your subconscious working perfectly in sync with the universe as events unfold that facilitate you manifesting these long-held desires.

What can't be repeated too many times at this point of your planning is that you must take the first step. You can take it tentatively and hesitantly, that's fine. You can take action with a small measure of doubt that you're actually taking the correct action. The truth is as long as you take action it's the right action.

If it should be the wrong step, your subconscious mind and the universe will work together to set you on the proper path. Guaranteed!

Exercise 3: Use Positive Affirmations to Nourish your Subconscious Mind

This exercise practically goes hand in hand with the previous one. Using those goals you've written, write out positive affirmations that will help you achieve those goals. You're going to create affirmations that, above all, are written in the present tense even though you may not have seen these goals met yet.

For example, I have a friend who has one affirmation. I am a New York Times Best Selling author. She isn't, not yet there. But as you recall her subconscious can't tell the real world from the imagined world. As she recites these words throughout the day, she visualizes what it would feel like to be a bestselling author.

The combination of the spoken and written word as well as projecting her emotions into the situation will eventually propel her to that status.

Decide on one or two areas you'd like to work on first. Review your list of goals and create a positive, present tense affirmation to suit your specific needs. This is now yours. Write it out daily and be sure to speak it daily. Yes, especially in the morning when you wake up and in the evening as part of your ritual before you retire.

Believe it or not, you've now created another habit of the successful person. Continue to do this. You may only want to concentrate on one or two affirmations at a time so you can truly focus on them. Congratulations.

In the chapters that follow, we're going to learn more about the laws of the universe, how they work and especially how you can use these to create habits of success and prosperity. But in the meantime begin to put everything you've learned up to now into practice. Your excitement will only mount as you begin to see how your mind is beginning to stir up the long-buried dreams and goals.

Are you ready to continue your success journey? There's no time like the present.

CHAPTER 3:

❧

DEVELOPING THE MINDSET OF A SUCCESSFUL PERSON

R eally," Jim said to Zach one day, "what good is all this indoctrination. Do you really think that the universe will change its ways just because I've changed my view of it? Do you really think that if I establish these habits that'll make any difference?

"The wheels of my future were set in motion a long time ago. Maybe even before I was born. The universe isn't about to bow down to my way of thinking just because I tell it to. Let's face it, those no magic genie coming out of a magic lamp to propel me to success. I can't change the past.

Jim didn't really know how far off the mark he was. Once you begin using these awesome universal laws, you'll feel as if you're unleashing a genie from a magic lamp. If every any entity had ever said, "Your wish is my command," it's the remarkable energy flow of the universe.

Even if you can't technically change the past, you can turn your present moment around and you'll discover how to use its power to create a better and more successful life – much more quickly than you ever thought possible.

So what are these four rules you need to follow?

1. Take total responsibility for your life.

> *"Man must cease attributing his problems to his environment, and learn again to exercise his will – his personal responsibility."*
> **Albert Einstein**

I can hear you now. "But it really wasn't my fault. I was in the wrong place at the wrong time. Everybody else has done things like that. But I'm the one to get caught. I was born under the wrong stars."

It doesn't really matter what argument you've decided to use, the bottom line is, your protests are probably merely excuses, so you can absolve yourself of at least some of the pain of not creating a successful life and not developing better habits sooner in your life.

Over the years, if you're like most of us, you've tried to push the blame for various events. A popular excuse is even the saying of "Life happened while I was making other plans." It's such a common excuse (and yes, that's all it is) that it's accepted by just about everybody as a legitimate argument.

But upon closer inspection, you'll discover that this is merely another one of those excuses to absolve yourself of the responsibility for your own happiness, for your own success.

If you've done this, don't believe for a moment that it's not too late to change your change the way you think and some to believe you really do control not only your thoughts but your actions as well.

In fact, by beginning step by step changing your habits from bad to good, can start right now to take full control of each and every action in your life. Before you even begin to argue, remember that this full confession is one of the most important steps you can take in beginning to feel good about your life.

Besides, if you don't do this, you'll go through life believing that you don't have full control over the events you're experiencing. Let me rephrase that. You may not have full control of everything that happens to you, but you have absolutely full control over how you react to those events.

This small change in perception can – and with time will – bring about a major transformation about how you view life and the amount of "luck" you'll need to get through it.

The Power of A Brand New Start

Reassess these events impartially. Instead of blaming luck, analyze them constructively from the viewpoint of what you may have done differently in order to take full responsibility for that situation at that moment.

Once you've done that, and realize what you could have changed your next step is to remember what could have been done and forget about continuing to blame others or the "stars" or conjuring it as a part of fate. Instead, remember what you could have taken responsibility for. Then the next time you encounter a similar situation, be sure to take control of the event.

No one said it was going to be easy. But going forward you'll discover it's worth it. Don't make a big deal of it if you happen to slip up. Everyone does now and then. As soon as you realize you're not taking responsibility for whatever it is, then vow to start again and tighten control of the situation.

Yes, relinquishing your responsibility would be so much easier, less painful and, indeed, much less demanding. It's also a much more comfortable approach. You can just sit back and point a finger at Aunt Katie, or your mother or your friend, Kevin. "It's their fault I'm not a greater success," you can say smugly.

Once again you can end your day by sitting in your living room, watching television while you munch on a bag of microwave popcorn mumbling to yourself, "When will life ever give me a break?"

But think of the power you're allowing others to have over your life. Think of the power you're handing to the "whimsical" fate of the universe.

2. Discover Your Purpose

Those individuals who have a problem taking control of their life and responsibility for their own successes (and failures) usually have another trait in common. They're not sure what their purpose in life is.

Why of course not. You're never going to understand what the Universe wants you ultimately to do with your time on earth if you're constantly giving away your responsibility. Have you ever met someone who constantly says, in response to what she was planning for the day, "I'm going to let the events unfold as they want"?

That's all well and good. Up to a point. It shows some degree of sensibility, but more than that is that it shows a fear of stepping up to the home plate, looking the pitcher in the eyes and then hitting that ball he throws at you out of the ballpark.

Every time you allow the universe to unfold and fail to make plans, the universe will find some excuse for you not to do much of anything that day – or get caught up in the drama of others.

The truth of the matter we all have to be attuned to the direction the universe tugs us. But by the same token, we need to take responsibility (there's that phrase again) and step out. It's the only way that you'll be able to read the events and actually figure out what it is the universe really wants you to do.

3. Decide What You Want

And, yes that's the next step in the process of using these amazing laws of the universe to your advantage. As you read about these irrefutable laws, you'll discover that you've been using them all along – even if it means it's been to your detriment. Remember that your subconscious doesn't care what you feed it – optimism, pessimism, negativity, positivity – it'll process whatever thoughts you feed it. Then it magically, mystically (so it appears) manifests it into reality.

If you don't know what you want and you don't think steadily about your "purpose" in life, no wonder you haven't found your purpose yet.

4. Believe that Your Goals and Desires are Attainable.

By now, I've hoped I knocked you out of your comfort zone enough to get you picking up a pen and writing down some goals. Perhaps they're things you've always wanted to do but never found the time. Notice that turn of the phrase: found the time. You'll never find the time. You have to make the time. Again, you must take control.

Now's the time to decide what your goals, your desires, even those fleeting daydreams are possible. Always keep in mind the adage Henry Ford lived by: "Whether you believe it's possible or not, you're right."

CHAPTER 4:

❧

THE UNIVERSAL LAWS OF SUCCESS

A s Jim learned more about changing his habits, Zach began telling him more about the unseen laws of the universe that work in conjunction with the subconscious mind. Jim, however, was hesitate to accept the reality of these laws. "Look, Zach," he said, looking at his friend in the eye, "we've been friends too long for you to start giving me a load of nonsense. Don't you think if all these laws were real, we would have learned about them somewhere in our education?"

Our friend, Jim, brought up an excellent point. We don't learn about these as part of our education. We're allowed to grow up and enter the real world ignorant of the one thing that may make a gigantic difference in the way we not only view life, but live it as well. And this is where many individuals step in remaining skeptical even after they've been introduced to all the laws – or even the major ones.

Another reason many prefer to ignore these laws is that you can't see them at work as easily as you can see Newton's laws of physics at work. That doesn't mean they don't exist though.

Depending on who you're talking with, you may notice that they have a different count of how many universal laws exist to work with your subconscious mind. In reality, there is one – and every other law is really a merely a corollary to that. What is the overriding, supreme law which guides every other mental law? It's the Law of Attraction. If you're not that familiar with this rule, here's a quick overview of it.

The Law of Attraction

Just about everyone has heard about the law of attraction these days. In a nutshell. It says that you attract into your life what you think about all day long. You . . .

You're already interrupting the words and you haven't even read the entire explanation yet. But, it's not hard to guess what you're thinking. You're going to say you think about wealth, money and success all day long and the universe has yet to deliver any of that to you in a sufficient amount.

Consider what your thoughts were really telling the universe. Let's use an example of what happens in your mind throughout the day. Imagine you had a gnome-like creature following you every day, recording all of your thoughts. According to some experts, we average approximately 64,000 thoughts daily. If this gnome were to read your thoughts back to you at the end of each day. How many of these thoughts would be positive? How many would be affirming and re-affirming your desire to be wealthy and successful?

If you're much like any of us, you'll say you're affirming your wealth and financial success. But if you scratch under the skin, you'll discover that you're really not giving much attention to wealth, but to your lack of wealth. Oh sure, you're probably paying homage to your affirmations through reciting them and even writing them several times daily. Let's say, for the sake of argument, your spending two hours a day doing this.

While many individuals believe they're using their "power of positive thought" in this process and should be, any minute, attracting what they've been thinking about for that hour or so a day. But the rest of the day, as the transcription gnome testifies, who's been by your day all day says otherwise. You've been spending the other 20 hours on negative thinking. You're still filling your mind with ideas with negativity and the "craziness" of you even thinking you could be wealthy or successful by any standards.

What do you expect you'll manifest in your life? Wealth and success? Or more lack? Bingo! You're right! You'll attract more lack because overall those are your thoughts. Unfortunately, in this case, the law of attraction is busy at work providing you with exactly what you don't want: lack.

The law of attraction, as well as every other universal law, work through your subconscious mind. What is the first law of the subconscious? It doesn't judge any thought you give it. This aspect of your mind gives you exactly what you've been thinking about.

When you complain that the law of attraction isn't working in your life, dig deeper to try to decide what you've been feeding it. Instead of blaming the law of attraction try to impartially analyze what you've been thinking. That is probably where the snag is. The mind is providing you with exactly what you've been pondering all day long.

But the bottom line continues to be one of doubting the flow of wealth into your life. Just ask that gnome that's following you around keeping score of your thoughts.

One way to work around this problem is to visualize yourself successful and wealthy or whatever goal you'd like to see manifested. But you'll do a bit more than just that. As you see yourself in your mind's eye as successful, imagine what kind of feelings go with that kind of success.

Think about what you would feel like the moment you look at your bank account and you realize you really are wealthy. How would you feel? If you're like me, you'd probably be bouncing off the walls. Conjure up the emotions that go with this event in your life.

Now you're giving something the universe it can work positively with. Your subconscious mind doesn't work just with your thoughts. It can pick up on your feelings as well.

Remember, too, that your subconscious can't tell the real from the imagined. Think about it and use this fact to your advantage. If you're rich, even if you're not quite there yet, the universe will without a doubt pick on this, not even asking if it's an uplifting emotion from a real event or from your imagination.

That's one way of making a path for the law of attraction into your life. There are several other ways as well. One of the methods is by putting the many corollaries of the law of attraction into work.

The Law of Allowing

Yes, in many ways the law of allowing is much what it sounds like. Many individuals, especially those just starting out using these universal methods find it difficult that they actually work. That, along with the fact, that you may be trying to change ten, twenty years or more of your habit toward believing that you'll never attract the good in your life can remain a barrier to true success.

That's when we have to take a good long look at ourselves and study why we're not "allowing" ourselves to not only pass on some of the greatest moments of your lives but what we can do to change that around.

When many individuals are faced with making this turnaround in their lives, their first reaction is that they must do something immediately to change their thinking, to change their focus. Tell them, though, when they accept the presence of this law, they need to do little else, they're incredulous.

"You get absolutely nothing in life unless you work for it," people are prone to respond in these cases. The law of allowing though is actually the easiest way to manifest your needs and desires into reality.

Once you're visualizing your success and feeling it down to the core of your being, you've practically completed your end of the bargain. Of course, you're going to take action based on these feelings, but even here, the universe will be more than happy to deliver what you need and want.

We've been taught (in some instances it's been pounded into our heads) that we have to work hard for everything we receive in this world. That's fair enough, but have you ever had "good fortune" just fall into your lap? This is what it feels like to work with the law of allowing.

What you'll usually find happens during this process is that you'll take a few initial steps and then – viola! – the universe matches you step by step. Let's say you're trying to start a business, but what you need first is an investor. You ask around --- taking that initial step – the next thing you know, your friend suddenly remembers that a friend of his used a venture capitalist to help fund his project. Not only that, he'd be more than happy to have you two meet.

The next thing you know, you're signing a deal. You're on your way to having your business – your dream – funded. That's usually how the law of allowing works. If you find yourself working too hard at searching for a funding agent or any other component that you need, take a step back and ask if you're really "allowing" the powers that be, as it were, to work.

You've probably been taught you have to work hard for everything you receive in life. So when something like the above scenario occurs, it's almost too good to believe. But believe it anyway – and get used to it. Because when you add the law of attraction to the law of allowing – this is exactly what you receive.

Just because you've been told you have control over your destiny doesn't mean it requires you to bang your head against the wall in order to experience it. Just allow it to happen. Think about a sailing boat. Once you've lifted the anchor (taken the first step) you don't go telling the universe which way the wind should blow (or do you?). Instead, you step back and allow the wind to blow you and your vessel in one direction for a while. If you find you need to make some adjustments, you take the rudder and fine-tune your ship.

To be completely honest it really is a difficult concept to accept. The human ego wants to take credit for all of our accomplishments and so it wants to be busy "micromanaging" everything we do.

Practicing this law will eventually bring you face to face with the next law of universal good: the law of resistance. You can make an educated guess what this implies. Let's explore this topic in more detail in the next couple of paragraphs.

The Law of Resistance

So far, the names of these universal laws (which by the way, every successful person knows about) are aptly named for the results they bring into your life. In a nutshell (and in no way to sound flippant about it) what you resist is what persists.

Many individuals don't understand why that should be. While probably no one really knows for sure, it's a good bet that if you're resisting about it, you're placing a great deal of energy around it. When you do this, you're working with the law of attraction. And the universe and your subconscious mind with work together to give you exactly what you're thinking about. Which is precisely what you don't want.

For some individuals, especially for those who haven't quite adapted to using the law of attraction, this becomes a sign that they aren't met to have this. Others, who have encountered this probably before will consider the obstacle a bump in the road and take the initial steps to work around it.

And we all know what happens when we take action – even a little bit of action – the universe will help us out. Guaranteed. So, when you meet this resistance you shouldn't dwell on it.

Accept that something is blocking you and turn your subconscious mind on to find ways to overcome it. You may want to focus more on your positive affirmations to visualize more, revving up your feelings and emotions. Your subconscious mind will definitely react to that.

Then there's the one individual who stands in her bedroom, closes the door and yells at whatever powers that be (or herself): "You can't stop me! I am going to succeed, so you might as well join me!"

The Law of Detachment

If you've ever studied Buddhism or read anything about it, then you're probably familiar with this Universal Law. It's a tenant of Buddhist thought. That doesn't mean, however, that it's a strictly spiritual law.

In its basic form, this law says to put all of your desire into your goal, but then back away and remove yourself emotionally from the final outcome of the goal. This doesn't mean you don't care. It's closer to the idea that you're neither dev-astated nor overly elated depending on the out-come.

Before you begin to complain about it, you need to know that many people who never thought they could either enact this law, understand it or carry it through to its finality have found satis-faction in it.

For starters, they say, the law of detachment is liberating. You cast your goals into the ether and then simply let go of it, knowing that the Uni-verse is taking good care of it.

Perhaps the real advantage of this law, however, is that once you let it go, you're not second-guess-ing yourself and most importantly you're not fill-ing your emotions with negative thoughts and doubts. In other words, once you let it go, you can completely bypass that law of resistance.

You've already seen how even one negative thought can easily snowball into a couple more and with enough time passed you're showering your goal with negativity and worry. You know what happens then.

Have you created a goal or two yet? Are you beginning to feel any of the following emotions?

- Desperation

- Emptiness

- Anger

- Longing

If you are, then, you're cloaking your goal or desire with types of negativity. This makes it all the harder for your subconscious to work at manifesting your goal.

Here's a statistic to show why strictly following this universal rule of thumb is vital. Seventy percent of people find it much easier not only to accept the possibility of a negative outcome than believe they'll receive a positive one.

This fact really makes you wonder if as human beings, our brains are not hard-wired to think negative thoughts.

The Law of Abundance

This is one rule of the universe that many of us can't believe. That's because everything we've learned as children and taken to adulthood run counter to this concept. Even our economy is constructed based not on abundance, but scarcity. When people are introduced to this idea, they are a bit taken aback – to say the least.

The law of abundance, as its name implies dictates that there is more than enough of everything in the world to go around. Not only that, but the more of whatever it may be you share with others, the more will eventually be returned to you.

When you were growing up you probably heard the saying "Love is the only thing you can give away and always get more of." Don't believe it. This action, giving away what you have, sharing your possessions, money or whatever with others, is the quickest and surest way to ensure that you'll never run out of that particular item.

If you donate money to a good cause or give it strings free to another person, you'll eventually find that amount – plus more – return to you. It seems like an incredulous notion, but it's, indeed, true. Many people have started out skeptical, but gave it a try anyway and have been pleasantly surprised.

One person, who practiced this concept asked one day, "Why do you think we call money currency?" When the other person shrugged his shoulders, she answered, "because it's supposed to flow through us to others. If you do this, as you look upstream you'll see even more of the current bringing you even more money."

Difficult as it is to believe, you really do need to test this law out for yourself. Discover the satisfaction of giving money to others and the equally delightful feeling of it returning to you in the most unexpected of ways.

You'll only experience the law of abundance in your life when you believe – and not just give lip service to – that you have absolutely everything you need to complete your life and make you happy this very moment. You don't need one more penny for happiness. You don't need your dream home to be happy. You don't need to fall madly in love with your soul mate.

The moment you know deep in your soul that you're complete just the way you are, then the marvelous effects of the law of abundance will cascade upon you.

In fact, according to this rule, you have more than enough to supply all of your needs and wants. Brian Tracy, a well-known motivational speaker puts it simply, "You can have virtually all you need and want." You merely have to take the first step of deciding that this is what you want.

More often than not people make a certain amount of money in life and then suddenly put a limit on that. They believe for whatever reason, that's all they should be making. Some individuals believe they're not worth any more than what they've established in their minds.

To paraphrase Marianne Williamson another motivational and spiritual speaker, too many of us ask "Who am I to be successful? The real question should be "Who am I not be?"

The first step is to decide what you truly want. People become wealthy, so the saying goes because they decide to become wealthy." It's that simple. Having made the decision to become wealthy, they then act in a manner that will produce that outcome – which includes adopting the good habits that propel them to success.

There's a flip side to this concept and that is that those without wealthy are poor because they haven't made the decision to become wealthy yet. Think about it. This type of thinking strips bear any excuses you may have been hiding behind in your present state. Not wealthy? Always blame it on not getting that "break" that others seem to get? No, you can't do that anymore.

Always blame your inability to make more money than what you're making right now on the economy or lack of resources or . . . stop it. Because right now, you know you're not wealthy simply because you haven't truly made the decision.

Stop reading this book for one moment and ask yourself this question, "Why aren't you rich yet?" Now get a pen and paper and write down every reason you believe you're not wealthy. Check them over carefully. Ask yourself one more question, "Are these legitimate reasons or are they merely excuses." Maybe up until the moment you began reading this book you believed they were reasons. It may be now you see them as excuses.

Using the Law of Abundance to Your Advantage Right Now

There's no time like the present! Realizing that, you also need to know that you can start right here and now to implement some of the most effective habits this very moment that will propel you on the road of success using the law of abundance. And believe it or not, it's much easier than you would ever guess.

Your first step is to imagine that every interaction you've ever had with money in some way came your way in order to teach you a special lesson about wealth. That being so, ask yourself what was the most important lesson you believed you've learned.

Your second step is to ask yourself what is your largest block of obtaining wealth. Answer this question and then act as if this block doesn't exist anymore. Eliminate this self-limiting action and the belief from which it stems and you'll discover how quickly you'll begin to propel yourself towards the road of wealth.

The Law of Action

You undoubtedly knew that we'd end up talking about action in some form. After all, what are habits but actions you take practically subconsciously? Habits are actions that you do without thinking. So, it only makes sense that a corollary to the Law of Attraction would be one dealing with action.

Unfortunately, many people, have a difficult time grasping the law of attraction and therefore tend to ignore its corollary. "It all seems too easy," many say, "What are you telling me? I wish upon a star and all my dreams come true?"

The way the law of attraction has been explained by misinformed people themselves, but the steps you need you to take after you invoke have never been clearly delineated. One of the most important steps you can take in manifesting your goals is through action.

That's why the more good habits of the success you can adopt, the more successful you'll be. In its simplest terms, the law of action says that nothing happens until you take that first step toward your goal. Action, in effect, kick-starts the entire process.

Very often the law of attraction is compared to planting a seed. You plant a seed and it grows. If you plant a bean seed, for example, you'll get – you guessed it – a bean. It doesn't get much simpler than that, does it?

Imagine a farmer sitting on in a rocking chair on his back porch, just staring out at the field, rocking away. Soon, his wife comes outside to visit him. "What are you doing?" she asks him.

"Waiting for my field of corn to grow," he answered, not taking his eyes off the field.

"I don't recall you planting corn in that field," his wife said. "In fact, I don't recall you planting anything in that field."

"Nope," he said, "I didn't plant anything there."

"If you didn't take the initial step of planting, nothing will grow," his wife said, adding, "isn't that one of those fundamental rules of farming?"

"I'm visualizing," he snapped back. "I heard in one of those self-help books that all you need to do is think about what you want out of life and write down your goals."

His wife got up from her chair and walked inside shaking her head. "It's going to be a long growing season," she mumbled to herself.

Ironically, no one asks why corn isn't growing in that field. No seed. No crop. It's just that simple.

Yet many individuals sit in that chair (or on the couch watching television) waiting for a business to grow. Imagine someone visits the person on the couch, asking him what he's doing. "Waiting for my business to grow," he says, not taking his eyes off the television.

"I didn't know you had a business," his friend comments.

"I don't right now," he said proudly, "but I will soon. I invoked the law of attraction. Before you know it I'll be attracting wealth through the visualization I've been doing. Something will surely happen and soon. I hear it's guaranteed. Right now, in fact, I'm engaged visualizing my business."

What do you think the odds are his method of growing business will actually produce anything – except a greater understanding of the latest crime show.

When you've made your mind up to start a business, it's so much easier to invoke the corollary of the law of action if you've already adopted even a few of the good habits associated with the highly successful.

Even if you haven't adopted any habits, though, that doesn't mean you can't succeed. But you'll never succeed just by wishing it so. You need to take action and the sooner the better.

Create your Very Own Fantasy World . . .

. . . And watch it manifest into reality!

As you lay in bed each night, before you fall asleep, begin to visualize what your life would be like if you could spend all of your days doing whatever you want. Right now, no part of your fantasy has to be related to your goals. Just think about what you would do if you could be doing anything at all at this very minute?

Would you be writing that bestselling novel? Or would your thoughts and energy turn to a tropical beach doing yoga? Or just relaxing on that beach? Some individuals opt to wander around their dream home, seeing it in their mind's eye as detailed as possible.

You already know from our previous conversation that you're tapping into the power of your subconscious mind as you do this. You also know your subconscious mind can't tell the difference between reality and imagination. So if you "conjure" up your imagined world, it slowly becomes more of a reality to your subconscious.

This experiment works best when you stay in your fantasy as long as you possibly can. Do this every night and you'll discover that this place of escape will indeed become your "happy place." You'll not only find it comforting, but you'll also look forward to visiting it. Before you know it, the creation of a fantasy world has become a habit.

Take this Habit to the Next Level

This habit – performed by many of the most successful executives around -- in and of itself is invaluable to your future. But what if you carried this out a bit farther? Once you've created your fantasy world, your next step is to take one item you've been worrying about – just one – and think about it. Now visualize the best possible outcome for this worry.

For example, I know one person who worried about a bill that she couldn't pay at the moment. So, one night, she decided that she would use the principle of this habit to visualize that bill being paid. She imagined not only herself paying the bill but how she would feel once this burden was lifted from her.

She continued creating this scenario for several nights in a row. Before she knew it a combination of events occurred in her life that she was able to pay off that debt. This awesomely effective habit is the best possible example of these universal laws at work. Painlessly and effortlessly.

Now, you're going to learn the ultimate utilization of this exercise. When you turn this underused technique into a habit, you'll be unleashing a resource known at the moment only to those who are the most successful.

Transfer this nightly habit and wake up fully intending your new-found talent for visualizing. Get yourself seating into a comfortable pose, similar to those individuals use when their meditating. In a very real sense, you'll be meditating over your day – with an eye to giving a positive spin on it.

Once you're seated and your eyes are closed, imagine in as much detail as you can, the events of the day ahead. Where do you start? At the very beginning, with a healthy breakfast if you want. You may want to start envisioning an anger-free commute to work.

Then go through the details of your day as you would like the events to play out. If you have a meeting with an important client, imagine the meeting being beneficial to both of you. Continue playing out your day ahead of time. Think about how wonderful your afternoon will be. Visualize yourself going through all the motions, from answering the phones to interacting with your office.

Here's the best part of the habit though. When you get through imagining through the end of the day, feel how happy you'll be. Feel the same emotions you'd have if your day really went that smoothly. Soak in those emotions for a while before you break your meditation.

Do this regularly. See how this improves your days. Notice if your productivity doesn't increase. You'll be surprised how it affects your mood as well.

Working alone on your goals is a powerful method of carrying out your dream. There is a method, however, you can use to make the power of visualization even more potent. It's called a Mastermind group. If you've never heard about one before you're in for an eye-opening example of the synergistic power of a group.

If you have heard of this classic example of the power of the mind at work, but have never thought of joining one before, I certainly hope you seriously consider finding one to join or start your own group.

Ready to learn more about this awesome group? The following chapter is devoted to Masterminding.

CHAPTER 5:

❧

THE POWERFUL HABIT OF A MASTERMIND GROUP

I f you have heard of Mastermind groups prior to this, you may have thought of them as a support group. But they aren't. Most support groups are aimed at people overcoming a singular disease, addiction or trauma. Probably about the most well-known of these is Alcoholics Anonymous. There are also groups that help cancer patients get through their treatments or even groups for those experiencing Post Traumatic Syndrome Disorder.

All of those organizations help people cope with their present situation to help you deal with life as you meet it head-on. A Mastermind group differs in that it's designed to propel you forward.

It's all about enabling you – and your partners in your group – in

working toward a dream or achieving your goal.

Having said that, don't think for a moment those observations about support groups are meant to malign any of them. They are extremely important and in many ways are, indeed, propelling those participants to success. But Masterminding offers a different kind of support.

Don't think it has to be an enormous or even elaborate goal you bring to your group for aid. Some individuals join a Mastermind group solely to work toward their goal of working toward an "authentic" life. In very simple terms the group is designed to propel you toward something in the future, not about healing you from past events.

While this sounds like an easy enough task, this is exactly the reason many Mastermind groups fail. Some members eventually start slipping into a different mindset.

Before you decide to either start one or to join such a group, remember that it requires quite a bit of positive energy. You're not only trying to provide yourself with a booster shot of optimism and positive energy, but you're also holding that same level of energy for others in your group.

2. A Mastermind group is a "no whining zone"

Seriously, it is. No single person should dominate the conversation trying to conduct a "pity party." Technically speaking, no person should dominate the conversation at all.

Each individual present should get roughly the same amount of time to present his or her vision of the future to the group. This is the time to quickly talk about your goals, dreams and the challenges that accompany the achievement of them.

The concept behind a Mastermind group is creating a mindset for success. That can't be done if members are allowed to whine about problems. Remember the law of attraction. What you think about you bring into manifestation.

Before you enter your group, get yourself mentally prepared for an exciting, energy-expending time. Not only will you be excited about the events in your future, a large part of this group is creating and maintaining excitement for your partners' projects as well.

3. An effective Mastermind group will pull you out of your comfort zone.

If you haven't discovered this concept yet, creating success is difficult if you refuse to step out of your comfort zone. You can't build a career as a novelist if you prefer to spend your days avoiding pen and paper or your computer. That's not going to get you to the level of success you hunger for.

If you're truly honest with yourself, you'd admit that's exactly what you're trying to do – jump out of your comfort zone. You'll discover during this time you'll live beyond it, as well as make future plans that should keep you out of it for a while longer. Mastermind groups are potentially effective because they force you to push you past your old limits. They surprise you with how far you can take your new limits.

4. Mastermind is synonymous with account-ability

Every time you attend a session, you're part of a culture of accountability. You become responsible for your own success. You can't walk in and blame the alignment of the stars for your not succeeding. You can't give any vague excuses for not meeting your next goal.

You may be moaning about it at this point, but give it a try. You'll discover that it's the best thing you can do for your career and goals.

5. The successful Mastermind group creates ideas and manifests resources

That sounds like almost an impossible task for several people who are all living different lives propelling themselves toward their individual successes. But believe it or not it's true and it has worked for an amazing number of individuals

Don't chalk this up to dumb luck. Because that's not the reason a host of various actions and ideas erupts in these groups. It's the synergistic power of many focusing – even for a few moments – on the dreams, goals, and intentions of another person. Okay, it may sound corny. It may sound hokey. Call it anything you like. But the bottom line is that it works.

It's at this very moment that the law of attraction kicks in and connections are uncovered and resources revealed. It usually is not only helpful for that individual, but others in the group may have that "eureka" moment and a gem within the conversation that they can mine.

6. There's a mystical element to a Mastermind session.

Person after person has commented on this. There is, indeed, a mystical element to these meetings. You may consider this a bit odd because your group had no intention of creating a mystical or even spiritual group when you formed it.

But the longer you and your partners are together as a group, asking the universe to lead you to your next step to success, the faster you'll discover these requests are fulfilled. It's part of retraining the subconscious mind to listen to you. Another reason your requests seem to get a swifter response the longer you do it is that you're reprogramming your subconscious mind.

Those are the basic tenets of any good Mastermind session. As the steps indicate, you may discover that the group starts off a bit slow. Answers to your requests, manifestation of even the smallest of your goals may take time. But as you begin to work with the group members, your subconscious mind and the universal laws, you'll discover that you're not so much requesting as you are doing positive affirmation.

You'll soon learn that all you need to do is claim your good. The moment you decide on your path, the universe and the amazing power of your mind go to work in making it happen.

In addition to using the universal laws and building a Mastermind group, successful individuals practice a host of positive habits that help to usher in and sustain their success. In the following chapter, you'll discover how to create the habits of the highly successful. Once you know how to create and establish these, you'll find that your journey to success will be kicked into overdrive.

CHAPTER 6:

✦

THE MOST EFFECTIVE WAY TO BUILD A HABIT

*A*ttraction. Intention. Action.

Zach and Jim continued to talk occasionally about what made a successful person. They finally agreed on those three ingredients. "Not that there are so many more ingredients we could toss into this soup," Jim said. But now, he was clearly seeing that the world wasn't going to hand him success on a silver platter as it did to him, and so many others, in high school.

No, he now knew he would have to generate a certain level of enthusiasm and then to take appropriate action afterward. He gave it some thought and said, "Then I need to start creating new good habits that will contribute to my success and not sabotage me for my future goals.

He left the café determined to write out his goals and start creating new habits based on those goals immediately.

Smart man. The best action anyone can take – including you – is to create habits that will not only help you generate your goals but carry them out for years and years. These habits will become your secret weapons on your journey.

That's great, you say. But exactly how do you not only create a habit but ensure you're going to still be using them next month, next year and even farther down the road?

You've probably heard that if you take one action and perform it for twenty-one days, it becomes a habit. That's true. But to be truthful that's only part of the story. You need to make it as easy as possible on your subconscious to make a habit. Don't worry that you're making it "too easy" for yourself. Give yourself credit. You're actually asking quite of bit of your mind. Don't worry. It'll perform and excel with flying colors.

But it's going to take a few more techniques than merely performing one action for twenty-one days. That's what this chapter is all about. You're about to learn how the most effective and successful business people have done to train their brains to create habits that stick.

Your first task, though, is identifying the bad habits you've picked up over the years when it comes to your career and your life. Sure, it's easy to identify the bad habits that involve your health: smoking, lack of exercise, excessive coffee intake, eating too much junk food, becoming a couch potato at night and not moving from the sofa except to visit the junk food cabinet.

It's a bit more difficult to identify the poor work habits we've accumulated over time and even harder trying to correct them – especially when working alone. That's why you were given some information earlier about starting a Mastermind group. You'll want to include successful business mentors in your group not only so they can help you identify those habits which are holding you back, but to identify the ones you need to succeed and to implement into your lifestyle.

Brace yourself for a bit of concerted effort. While we're not saying that changing habits is necessarily easy, it will entail you to work at it some and above all for you to be patient with yourself.

Your bad habit didn't happen one day. It took a concerted effort and months of regular action to ingrain them into your system. It's going to take some time, effort and above all patience to kick them out and replace them with a habit that will kick-start and sustain your success – for the rest of your life, we may add.

Just listen to Christin Whelan, a public sociologist at the University of Wisconsin-Madison. She's an expert on the topic of habits currently working with AARP's Life Reimagined Institute. She's been studying happiness, human ecology and above all habits.

Making a lasting change in your life may take a few different forms. First, you may need to add an action to your life. Or it could be you need to end an activity you're currently doing. When you talk about being successful, you've got to first consider what it is you need to do.

Add a Habit . . . Subtract What?

It's easy to say I want to go to the gym for an hour and a half a day three days a week. But when you make this resolution, you seriously ponder what **is not going to get done during the hours we're at the gym.** Most individuals don't think about they're surrendering in order to add that awesome habit into their lives.

Before you make your vow to go to the gym, let's say, consider what it is that is not going to happen during those hours you're there. If you're like my friend, the freelance writer, you're taking yourself out of a minimum of two hours a day of what could be productive writing.

The question then becomes, "Is my time at the gym worth more than the loss of several hours of work? Or it maybe can I go to the gym at a time when it doesn't conflict with my productivity. Would I be willing to give up a couple of hours of sleep in the morning for my new-found habit of exercise?"

These are questions you need to ask before you enter into any agreement with yourself about starting a new habit. If you don't and you realize as my friend did that she really needed that time to write – at least on certain days – then she very well may not continue the habit.

Do you know what happened after that? She blamed herself for not having enough willpower to continue. That really wasn't exactly how all her habit ended it. She unnecessarily put the burden of a failed habit on an internal flaw of hers. She felt bad enough to begin with, she needn't start playing the blame game with herself.

How many times have you done the very same thing?

That's the reason some individuals avoid pledging chunks of time out of their workday, Dr. Whelen explains. Instead, the pledge to create commitment strategies. This may be the best way to establish a habit, she said. They hold themselves accountable, sometimes in public ways.

While this isn't always the best method of establishing a new habit it does indeed work for some people.

One of the most effective change strategies is to automate the change into your life. The aim of this is that you're incorporating the new behavior into your life with a minimum of thought.

After trying to put an effective exercise program into his life and experiencing what he felt was failure one individual hit upon an idea. He, just like every one of us, used the restroom every day – several times a day. He decided every time he went to the bathroom he vowed to do so many sit-ups. In this way, he didn't as if we're "stealing" anytime from his work, but he was still able to get a good number of sit-ups.

He was amazed at how quickly this became a habit and how much of a difference it made in his life.

Another friend of mine started meditating in the evening. She watched television and during the commercials, she muted the television and grabbed several minutes of meditation time during those quiet moments. Of course, instead of closing her eyes, she gazed at the television. When the program returned, she turned the sound back on and continued to watch the show.

She was getting all the benefits of meditation, without having to remember to set aside twenty or so minutes daily. If she added a longer session later in the evening, so much the better.

How long does it take to instill a habit?

If you've rattled off the number " twenty-one" you've confirmed what many people think, but Dr. Whelen is a bit more pessimistic about that. She affirms that to truly make a habit stick, you probably need to do it for a minimum of ninety days. The bottom line, she admits, is that you'll be more successful in creating a lasting habit, one you truly don't have to think about doing, the longer you continue to do it.

While this may sound like it's difficult to create good habits, you must remember you didn't fall into those bad habits overnight. The good news, though, is that once you've established this habit, the carrying out of it does indeed eventually become effortless. At some point, you'll discover that you're performing this action without any thinking involved.

It won't require self-control on your part or much active internal debate about it. You'll just find yourself doing it. At some point, it becomes a part of you. On those few days, you don't perform one of your habits, you'll feel something missing in your day – even if you can't identify it right away.

Below is a checklist that Dr. Whelen suggests you go through as you add new positive habits into your daily routine:

1. Take tiny steps. Choose one action at a time. Don't do an entire makeover.

2. Decide not only what you need to add to your routine to make this happen, but what you may

have to subtract from your daily routine. Then make room for it.

3. **Make sure you're creating a new positive habit because you want it, not because your spouse, mother or somebody else wants you to.**

4. **Get a partner, friend or family member to hold you accountable for continuing the habit, especially in those early days when you're in the position of pondering it.**

Is it getting up an hour earlier? Have someone at some time during the day contact you to see if you kept that commitment.

5. **If you must, tie this new habit to something you have to do anyway.**

In other words, automate it. Like the individual who tries his series of sit-ups with his restroom visits, you'll find it hard not to do after a while.

6. **Celebrate your continued success at certain intervals.**

What you choose to do is up to you, but don't forget to give yourself a pat on the back, in some form.

7. Stick with the habit.

The longer you continue to do it, the better the prospects it will become a part of you. Once it does become a routine, you'll notice when you skip it. But even better than that, the chances of you just "skipping it," will dwindle tremendously.

CHAPTER 7:

❧

BECOME AWARE OF YOUR SURROUNDINGS

Think back for a moment when you were a child. Your parents, grandparents or even your teachers may have said to you at one point, "Don't become friends with him. He's nothing but trouble. Did they ever warn you about keeping company with certain individuals because they'll certainly take you down the wrong road?

They probably worried about who your friends were. For many of us, it seemed so silly.

Your parents knew more than what they let on, however. They were only expressing themselves in good old-fashioned terms. But if you're seeking to be wildly successful at whatever you choose, you should once again be careful about how you choose your friends and acquaintances.

Today, psychologists believe that who you keep company with could indeed spell the death of your success in the business. That may be a bit of an overstatement, but not much. It's estimated that you are the average of the five individuals you spend the most time with.

Who are five of your best friends? Who in the course of your working hours, you spend the most time around? Who do you spend your off-hours from work with? List these five people and examine their attitudes. Are they optimistic or pessimistic or just indifferent to their surroundings?

Are they successful in their endeavors? Do they exemplify good habits?

Maybe in your pursuit of success and attaining your goals, you may want to add spending time with individuals who/ are more aligned with your thoughts, who are liable to more supportive of your goals, and ideally, have already been where you are and have turned the corner and are successes in their own right.

If you want to be an online marketer, then make it a point to meet people who have already launched successful websites. If you can't find any people to meet in person locally, find out where on the Internet people with your interests visit. Make it a point to engage others in conversations and to participate in ongoing conversations. You'll be surprised at how quickly and graciously people will help you out.

If you want to be an author, joining creative writing groups and professional organizations. Here you'll find not only those just beginning in the business but those who have already published a book. Soon, without you even realizing it you're absorbing and adopting some of the best habits of these individuals.

On the flip side, do you only spend time who think they're doomed even before they begin, who know for a fact it would be a waste of time to even start a business because the odds are stacked against them? Over time, their pattern of thinking may influence more than you'll know. You may, without even realizing it, began to adopt the same type of thinking and belief system.

If you're serious about success, then you really would be doing yourself a big favor if you begin to seek out and spend time with individuals who are already successful. Ideally, you'll want to spend time with those who have attained their goals. Ideally, you need to be spending more time with those who have made it in a career you're interested in.

If you're thinking you need a mentor at this point, you're almost there. These people will be mentors – and this is important – but they'll also at a deeper level become friends. They'll be those you most want to emulate. You'll be in a position to view up close and personal the habits that have taken them from where you are today to where they are today.

Meet Others of Like Minds

One of the best places to discover people like this – a whole roomful of individuals like this – is at a local Rotary Club. If you're a woman, you can also check out a local Business Woman's group. Both of these, and whatever other professional organizations you can discover that fit your niche, would be perfect for you.

At this point, may think you have to dump a specific number of your older friends who have bad thought habits, aren't encouraging and believe that any attempt at making something of yourself is a pie in the sky silly notion. That's just not so.

What you'll find occurring, though, is that as you progress in searching out more encouraging acquaintances, you'll have less in common with those whose thinking doesn't align with yours. It will be more of a parting of the ways because you and these more pessimistic individuals have less in common than ever before.

There's also another, far-reaching reason to spend time with professional people more in line with your interests. By doing so, you'll be able to identify two aspects of their actions that you can adopt as your own: their good habits which in turn will shed light on your own bad habits.

At this very moment, you may be saying you have no bad habits. And you may really believe it. It could be, though, you just don't recognize them either. Once you discover the actions, thinking patterns and habits of the successful, you may be better able to turn the light on your own habits you'd like to either replace or adopt.

Don't take this personally. Every person on this planet has some type of bad habit, even if it's only fueling their energy on caffeine. The odds are far more likely that even that person has more bad habits than he cares to admit. When you think of a bad habit, you only believe it deals with things you're now doing that are blocking your success.

Consider that a bad habit could just as easily be the omission of something you could be doing that would make you more successful. If you're not exercising, you may very well call this a bad habit – even though most people wouldn't say this.

If you're a part-time entrepreneur now and aren't getting up at four in the morning to add a couple of hours to your already harried day, wouldn't be called a vice by some. However to an individual who does wake up at four in the morning every day it is.

One of the biggest obstacles many of us encounter when we attempt to break a bad habit is that we attempt, merely just to quit doing it. We don't realize we've just created a void where an action used to exist.

One of the keys to help underline your success is to replace your bad habit with another action. This method recognizes that the laws of physics can't stand a vacuum. When you quit one habit, it's easier to fill that empty space – that vacuum – with some action. We've all met people who want nothing more than lose weight for example.

Some who try to quit smoking will naturally turn working crossword or Sudoku puzzles.

If you're trying to quit smoking, for example, you may be at a loss, especially at the initial changes of the process, because you don't know what to do with your hands. There are some individuals who recognize this and choose instead of smoking to buy a deck of cards and play solitaire at those times they were smoking instead. Or some individuals merely shuffle the cards, discovering that's action enough.

The key to adopting good working patterns and shedding the bad ones can be summed up in one simple phrase: *become aware of your surroundings.* If you've ever performed mindful meditation, then you know just what we're talking about. The first step is to become aware of them, but not to judge them. At least initially, they'll be a time and place you'll want to kick the bad working patterns to the street. When that time occurs, then there is a way you may like to do it.

1. Acknowledge and identify your bad habit.

As we discussed earlier, they'll come a time when you see that your waking up later than you think you should be is a bad habit that needs to be broken. Once you realize that, you're more likely to work at establishing a new morning routine that starts earlier in the day. After that, it's just a matter of time before you make that happen.

What is one of the most effective ways of acknowledging a bad habit for what it is? You may want to create and work with what many call an awareness log. It's a simple approach composed of a series of personal questions to heighten your awareness of when these habits are occurring. Exactly what kind of questions you ask yourself is going to depend on the habit you're trying to break.

Some of the questions you may want to ask yourself *include* these:

- Where are you when you get the urge to perform this habit? (Time and place)

- Does this urge occur at a certain time of the day?

- What is your emotional state? Tired? Depressed?

- Does this habit occur when you're with specific people? In other words, is the "average of five" kicking in? Are your friends bringing you down?

- Was there some action that occurred right before you got this urge?

2. Give yourself a deadline to begin your new behavior.

That's right! You've read that it's important to set a goal and give yourself a reasonable amount of time to reach it. It's also important, if not more so, to give yourself a target day on initiating the new pattern.

There's a very specific reason for doing this. You must make sure you – and your subconscious mind – are ready for this adventure. If you begin prematurely – especially if you're feeling you're coercing your body into this – then you'll probably setting yourself up for failure. And perhaps scarring your psyche.

3. Recognize the triggers

Many bad habits are triggered by performing other actions. You've probably heard people say they crave a cigarette the moment they have a beer or other drink in their hand. If you've ever smoked or drank, perhaps you have firsthand information about that.

Similarly, some individuals recognize that watching television triggers their desire to munch on junk food.

If you're trying to quit one habit, be sure you're aware that your toughest moments may be those in which you can't avoid a trigger. In fact, many experts tell you to take your time and make a list of those type of activities. In this way, you'll be able to identify them beforehand. But don't stop there, you'll want to have a reasonable game plan already in place so you're prepared – at the least not completely blindsided.

4. Work at your own pace.

The tendency when you start a new habit is to give yourself an elaborate new make-over. Many people tend to tackle all of their bad habits at one time. This practice can be exhausting. It can also be setting you up for failure.

Don't think about how many habits you can shed in the shortest amount of time. Think about the habit you believe is the one that's the largest obstacle to your success. You may want to do away with that one first. Or may want to dip your feet into the water with one of the minor bad work patterns you believe you have. Instead of trying to conquer them all, settle on cutting them down one at a time. Pull them up by the roots, so to speak. In this way, you're sued you've eliminated at least one of them

If you choose a single lesson first, then once you conquer this with relative ease, it'll build your self-confidence. In this way, you're also building momentum for more and greater changes.

5. Be prepared to forgive yourself.

Far too many individuals fail the first time they try to shed themselves on a bad working pattern and are fearful of starting over. Talk to anyone who has ever quit smoking and most of them will tell you that they tried several times before they were successful.

If you don't succeed on your first try, don't get discouraged. In fact, react with the opposite energy – increase your resolve to try again and succeed this time.

CHAPTER 8:

❧

MEDITATION: A HABIT OF 85% OF ALL SUCCESSFUL PEOPLE

J im and Zach were still sitting in the coffee shop talking about what made successful people. Zach commented that he recently acquired the habit of meditation. "It not only gives me a peace of mind at the end of the day," he told Jim, "but I start off every morning with a twenty-minute session. I can't tell you how much more I can get accomplished in a day."

Jim dismissed this idea as being off the wall. "I thought only the spiritually inclined and the stereotypical aging hippie meditated. Besides I don't believe in all that 'woo-woo' stuff."

Zach just smiled. He was about to let Jim in on the most well-kept secret of all successful business individuals.

In part, Jim is correct. Who among us doesn't associate meditation with another, earlier generation? After all, it was the famous rock group, *The Beatles,* who introduced most of the Western Culture to meditation some forty years ago.

But something amazing has occurred in those forty years since. Science has not only researched it but has certified it as being an effective healing resource. Not only can meditation heal your body, but it can also help your mind focus and become more productive.

Meditation is proving to be so powerful a tool and so amazingly beneficial, that some of the same skeptical scientists who are studying it are now practicing it themselves. And that's exactly what you want if you're looking to fulfill your career goals.

"Meditation more than anything in my life was the biggest ingredient of whatever success I've had."

You may think that sounds like the Dalai Lama speaking. Or even Oprah Winfrey. We've all come to expect that spiritual side to break through her business side now and then.

You'd be wrong on both counts. That's a quote from Ray Dalio. Who? That's the reaction of many. But Dalio is a billionaire and the founder of Bridgewater Associates, the largest hedge fund firm in the world. How's that for a model of a businessman who meditates?

But that's just one person, how about Rupert Murdock the chief executive officer of News Corp., the media mogul.

Today, you're just as likely to discover someone meditating in the boardroom of a Fortune 500 corporation than you are a local spiritual retreat.

Below are just a few more business people who have added the magnificent habit of meditation to their daily routine.

- Robert Stiller, CEO, Green Mountain Coffee Roasters, Inc.

- Tony Schwartz, CEO, The Energy Project

- William Ford, Executive Chairman, The Ford Motor Company

- Larry Brilliant, former director of Google.org

And we're not even about to list all the television and film celebrities who find it essential to their careers and peace of mind. The fact that so many outrageously successful business executives evidently find it an indispensable part of their daily habits should make you sit up and take notice.

Should You Meditate?

That's only a question you can answer. If you've seriously thought about meditating, this would be the time to start. If you've tried before and failed, don't allow that to keep you from trying again . . . and again . . . If you have to. The benefits you'll receive in improving your focus, boosting your productivity and turbocharging your concentration are that impressive.

Researchers have confirmed that the claims many individuals have made for years concerning the benefits of this habit really hold up. What can you expect when you begin your meditation program? No one can say for sure, but here's how it affects many others:

Greater Focus

For anyone who has already given meditation a try, this should come as no great surprise. That's the primary key to meditating, focusing on your breath. What may surprise you is that this ability to focus in on targets, much like a laser light, stays with you, even when you're not meditating. That focus lingers with us after we sit up and get down to work. Scientists now realize that focus can be strengthened like the muscles in your body. All you have to do is to exercise it.

Anxiety

It's true! The scientific reason for this is interesting and far more complex than can be explained here, but the bottom line is that, as far as researchers can detect, meditation loosens the connections of some of your neural pathways. This results in a more rational reaction when you're confronted with unsettling or unexpected sensations. You're much more likely to look at a potential business crisis with a calm demeanor instead of immediately envisioning the worst-case scenario.

Increased Creativity

Now, here's a trait everyone who is looking for success can use!

Those individuals who practiced a meditation technique called "open-monitoring" meditation, find that they have significantly increased their creativity. This type of meditation is also referred to at times as "awareness of thinking," or mindful meditation. Instead of sweeping all thought out of your mind, as you do in a focused session, you'll sit and be totally aware of your thoughts and feelings. Not only are you aware of them, but you're directed to observe them. Observe them, but don't judge them as either right or wrong, good or bad.

Some individuals believe this popular form quieting the mind allows the person meditating to become a "scientific observer" of sorts of his own mind. This means as you practice this you'll become increasingly aware of which thoughts actually trigger changes in your emotions.

In other words, you'll be able to tell what thoughts make you happy, which make you sad. Imagine being able to dissect your thinking. Then what do you think you can eventually do? You've got it, avoid those thoughts that bring sorrow or unnecessary sadness and concentrate on the thoughts can lift you up.

Once you start to feel the benefits of this wonderful habit, you may want to delve deeper into just how beneficial it can become in your life. If you enjoy the simple, mindful and focused versions of this activity, you may want to learn the more advanced versions, including conceptional and movement meditations. Unfortunately, we don't have the room to talk much about these types, but excellent descriptions and directions can be found in books dedicated to meditation.

Right now, let's get familiarized with a simple meditation that will get you up and running with this activity. The quicker you experiment with this, the quicker you'll know if it's an activity you want to adopt as a habit.

1. Select a mantra.

If you're not familiar with meditation, you may not be familiar with the word mantra. This is a word or a phrase you repeat to yourself while you're in session. The mantra is a great diversion to help you think about something else than your thoughts.

In a focused meditation, the goal is to sweep all thoughts of your mind. Your mind will try any trick in the book to try to push thoughts – any kind at all – back into your head.

What kind of phrase should you choose? Before you decide on your mantra, you may want to learn about some of the most popular ones. Some people use "peace" or "love." Some individuals even use something referred to as the "so hum" mantra. This is a sound typically used as a Sanskrit mantra, translated into "I am."

If you're a spiritual person who may have a number of words you may associate with peace of mind you'll want to use. If you're more secular, harmony, peace or love may be the most appropriate mantras.

2. Sit in a comfortable seat, in a quiet location.

It's best to find a quiet location, even if you have to lock yourself into your home office and place a sign on the door stating a meditation is in process. Once you adopt this as a regular activity, you don't want anybody to interrupt. Eventually, you'll also want to find a dedicated space for your sessions.

Right now, don't worry too much about where you're sitting. You may want to sit cross-legged on the floor with your back against a wall or on a chair or even a couch. The important thing is that you're comfortable. You'll also want to try to keep your spine as straight as possible. There are many individuals who choose to lie down during meditation. You may not want to do that during your initial learning stages. There's always that danger of your falling asleep.

3. Close your eyes. Take several "cleansing" breaths.

You're about ready to begin. Close your eyes. Take a breath, breathing through your nose. Exhale, breathing through your mouth. These are known as cleansing breaths. Once you've done this, then breathe normally through your nose. Keep your lips closed to ensure this happens.

4. Repeat your mantra silently to yourself.

The idea is to repeat your mantra silently. Don't force this repetition. Your mantra doesn't necessarily need to reflect the rhythm of your breath. If you like, you can connect the word to either your inhaling or exhaling, but that's not necessary. You'll recognize a successful meditation session when you're not forcing anything – no mantra, no breath, and it's not difficult to sweep away your thoughts.

5. At this point, don't focus on emptying your mind.

You're about natural, so don't get upset. You'll find there are times when you abruptly realize you're not reciting your mantra. "When did that happen?" you ask yourself. You discover you really can't tell when you stopped, but you did.

Stop! We all know what your first instinct is. Don't go there.

Instead of panicking and berating yourself, simply get back on course. Don't judge yourself for getting off track, to begin with. It happens to everyone now and then.

6. Continue if you can for five minutes.

Ultimately your goal for an effective meditation session will be twenty to thirty minutes. But when you're beginning, that's asking quite a bit of your mind. In fact, trying to sit this long on your first session may well be self-defeating. Your failure at remaining still for that long may mistakenly make you believe you're not capable of meditating. And that's just not true.

Considering the many benefits not only in your productivity but your health as well, meditation can bring, you shouldn't try it once and give up on it. That's not fair to you. Give it a try for several days, or better yet weeks. Keep in mind that the most recent research reveals that you're reaping all the benefits associated with this habit, even if you don't realize it.

Believe it or not, the benefits "sneak up on you." You may do this for several months and swear it's not helping you much. Then one day, you realize the time you've spent finally has paid off. So don't get discouraged.

CONCLUSION

"Thanks, buddy," Jim said to Zach as he pumped his hand. "My new career is taking off. And I couldn't have done it without you helping me identify and establishing a series of good habits. I appreciate the time you've spent with me."

Have you spent enough time on developing the new habits that you're off and running on your career? Hopefully, these pages are filled not only with suggestions that you'll read once but ideas and concepts you'll mine and adapt as your own.

If you haven't fully established all the habits you want, don't stop just because you've finished reading the book. Go back and review the habits you're still establishing. Review some of the laws that allow you to create the world of your dreams.

If you find your spirits sagging, don't allow yourself to even think about giving up. Convince yourself that giving up is not an option – because it isn't. If you open the door to walking away even an inch, you'll start relinquishing all the positive thoughts you've built up to this time. And before you know it, you really have given up, wondering what went wrong. You'll probably also end up kicking yourself later down the road.

So, keep this book handy, review it often and I'm betting you'll find new and creative ways you can put even a portion of these habits and laws to work for you. Not only that, but remember: When you're ready to take action, the universe will match you in guidance, nearly step by step.

But more than that, this book probably will propel you to go on to read more books on habits and success. That's great. The more knowledge you have the better equipped you'll be to continue on your journey.

You're only Laying the Foundation

Believe it or not, all the work that you've put into establishing good habits is really just the beginning. The work you've done so far has laid the foundation for future success. To continue your success, you'll find yourself not only perfecting these habits, but establishing an ever-expanding series of habits – one building on top of another – that will ensure that five years from now, you'll still be a major contender in whatever field you've chosen to work in.

Good habits never go "out of style." They'll never fail you. Once you've established your routine, trained your subconscious and are working harmoniously with the universe, then your accomplishments are unlimited.

Welcome to the world you were born to create for yourself!

Thank you for reading "Habits of The Super Rich". If you like and find this book helpful. Please take some time to share your thoughts and post a review. It'd be greatly appreciated.

I wish you the best and good luck!

Bruce Walker